W9-AQC-679

Date: 11/18/15

J 591.568 FRA
Franchino, Vicky,
Animal migrations /

Animal Migrations

VICKY FRANCHINO

Children's Press®
An Imprint of Scholastic Inc.

Content Consultant
Dr. Stephen S. Ditchkoff
Professor of Wildlife Sciences
Auburn University
Auburn, Alabama

Library of Congress Cataloging-in-Publication Data
Franchino, Vicky, author.
 Animal migrations / Vicky Franchino.
    pages cm. — (A true book)
 Summary: "Find out why animals migrate from one location to another, how they complete their journeys, and what difficulties they face along the way" — Provided by publisher.
 Includes bibliographical references and index.
 ISBN 978-0-531-21545-6 (library binding) — ISBN 978-0-531-21582-1 (pbk.)
1. Animal migration—Juvenile literature. 2. Migratory animals—Juvenile literature. I. Title. II. Series: True book.
 QL754.F72 2016
 591.56'8—dc23   2014049198

© 2016 Scholastic Inc.
All rights reserved. Published in 2016 by Children's Press, an imprint of Scholastic Inc. Published simultaneously in Canada. Printed in China 62
SCHOLASTIC, CHILDREN'S PRESS, A TRUE BOOK™, and associated logos are trademarks and/or registered trademarks of Scholastic Inc.
1 2 3 4 5 6 7 8 9 10 R 25 24 23 22 21 20 19 18 17 16

Front cover: Zebras and wildebeests climbing up a river bank during migration

Back cover: Monarch butterflies gather in Cerro Pélon in Mexico

Find the Truth!

Everything you are about to read is true *except* for one of the sentences on this page.

Which one is **TRUE**?

T or F   Migrations are always at least 100 miles (161 kilometers) long.

T or F   Humans have been able to teach a flock of birds to migrate.

Find the answers in this book.

Contents

THE BIG TRUTH!

The Serengeti-Mara Migration

Lantern fish

Monarch butterflies gather for a rest during their long migration.

Some sandhill cranes travel up to 300 miles (483 kilometers) a day.

CHAPTER 1

Traveling Times

As the days grow shorter, tourists arrive in Churchill, Manitoba. They have come to see the polar bears. These bears travel through this town in Canada each year as they **migrate** from their summer home to their winter one. During the summer, polar bears live on land and eat almost nothing. But as the temperatures drop and ice forms, they follow the ice and their favorite food: seals!

The best time to view polar bears in Manitoba is from October to November.

Short and Long Migrations

Each year, millions of animals fly, walk, crawl, slither, or swim from one place to another. Their migrations can be short or very long. The North American blue grouse lives in mountainous pine forests in the winter. It migrates just 400 to 1,600 feet (122 to 488 meters) lower in the spring. The tiny Arctic tern, on the other hand, flies 44,000 miles (71,000 kilometers) round-trip during its migratory journey!

Migrating "up" or "down" like the blue grouse does is called altitudinal migration.

A V-shaped formation of Canada geese heading south means winter is near.

Latitudinal and Seasonal Migration

There are many reasons animals migrate. When an animal moves north or south, it is called latitudinal migration. Animals that travel with changes in the weather are following a seasonal migration. Latitudinal and seasonal migrations often go together. For instance, Canada geese will fly north in the spring and south in the fall to find food and more comfortable temperatures.

European eels travel
from rivers to the ocean
each year to lay eggs.

Reproductive Migration

Animal mothers often move when it's time for their
young to be born. This is known as reproductive
migration. Sometimes a mother will move to an
area with a warmer climate or more food for her
and her babies. Other times she will move for
safety and protection. The mother will choose an
area where there are not so many predators or
where she has better shelter from them.

Nomads!

Animals do not always follow the same route or go to the same place every year. In fact, some animals seem to just be drifting without a plan! These **nomadic** migrators look for food or water and will wander until they find it. Some animals that usually stay in one place might be forced to migrate because of drought, flooding, fire, or other disasters.

African wild dogs spend most of the year as nomads, rarely staying more than a couple of nights in the same place.

Time to Migrate

How do animals know when the time is right to migrate? Scientists believe they might follow signs in nature. Shorter days, colder temperatures, and less available food could all tell animals that it is time to leave. Hormones can also be a trigger. Hormones affect how an animal's body grows, develops, and functions.

Emperor penguins migrate between their nesting site and areas with food.

Preparing for Their Trip

Humans prepare for a long trip by putting gas in the car and loading up on snacks. Some animals prepare for their long trips through a process called hyperphagia. This is a temporary condition when the animal's brain tells it to eat—and eat!—so it has fuel for its journey. An animal might increase its weight by up to 50 percent. Birds like the red knot (below) even have an increase in their heart size! This supplies strength and energy so the animal can survive the trip.

CHAPTER 2

Land Migrations

Animals travel without a map, compass, or **GPS** device. How do they navigate? Some animals gather clues from mountains, bodies of water, and other landforms. Other animals use their strong sense of smell to find places they have been before. Earth's **magnetic field** can also be a guide. Some animals even study the position of the sun and stars.

Salamanders use Earth's magnetic field to navigate.

Larger caribou herds often migrate farther than smaller herds, possibly to find enough food.

Long-Distance Travelers

Summer is coming and calves will soon be born. Before that happens, caribou herds must move north to find the nutritious plants they will need for their hungry babies. The females leave first, often traveling more than 600 miles (965 km). Males and year-old calves soon follow. The herd spends the summer eating their fill and moving shorter distances to avoid mosquitoes. By the time the first snows fall, the caribou are already heading south.

A Dangerous Journey

Caribou have the longest migration of any land animal in North America. Second place goes to pronghorns. Some pronghorn herds migrate in western Wyoming between the Upper Green River Valley and Grand Teton National Park. Round-trip, the journey is about 300 miles (483 km) long. The trip is hard. Pronghorns have to deal with predators and humans. Cars, fences, buildings, and roads often make it impossible for pronghorns to follow their migration route.

Pronghorns have to find a way around obstacles along their migration route.

17

Wriggly Wonders

The red-sided garter snake spends its first winter hibernating close to its birthplace. Every year after that, it will migrate to a larger den with thousands of its fellow snakes. In Manitoba, Canada, many of these snakes used to be killed as they traveled across roads during their migration. How was the problem solved? By having highway workers build small tunnels under the freeway!

Snakes, including garter snakes, find their den by "smelling" with their tongues.

Some elephants migrate for food and water. Others migrate to find a mate.

An Elephant Never Forgets

The oldest female member of a herd of Sumatran elephants has a very important job. She must remember the migration route for the entire herd! Sumatran elephants usually follow the same route every year, and they time their migration to avoid **monsoons**.

A Sumatran elephant's migration is usually shorter than an African elephant's. This is because water is more plentiful where Sumatran elephants live. They do not have to travel as far to find a good water source.

Today, bison live only in protected areas, parks, and ranches.

Wanderers No More

Until the 1800s, huge herds of bison migrated across the prairies of the central United States. A single herd could include up to 4 million individuals. Each year, herds traveled the few hundred miles between their summer and winter homes. They ate grasses and herbs along the way. However, bison were hunted nearly to **extinction** in North America during the 19th century. Though there has been some recovery, the bison population is still much smaller than it once was.

Getting to the Other Side

American toads wake up from their winter hibernation ready to migrate to their breeding grounds. Unfortunately, many have a big obstacle in their way: a road. As the toads try to cross busy roads that overlap with their migration route, they risk being hit by passing vehicles. Many toads never make it to the other side. Luckily, volunteers put up safety barricades and direct traffic to protect these amphibians and, later, their babies.

American toads usually migrate to the same breeding spot every year.

The Serengeti-Mara Migration

In the spring in East Africa, when the year's heavy rains are over and food sources have dried up, herds of wildebeests, zebras, and gazelles at Serengeti National Park must migrate to survive. They spend months traveling to the Masai Mara Game Reserve.

These animals are good companions and migrate together. Each type of animal eats different parts of the same plants. This means they do not have to compete with one another to find food.

Migrating in a group helps protect the animals from predators, but many still die along the way. Hyenas, lions, and cheetahs follow and attack the weakest members of the herds. Also, the herds must cross rivers at a time when the water is fast and dangerous. There, they face another threat: crocodiles!

In fall, the herds circle back to the Serengeti in time for the rains, which will bring new plant growth. In total, these animals travel nearly 2,000 miles (3,219 km) each year.

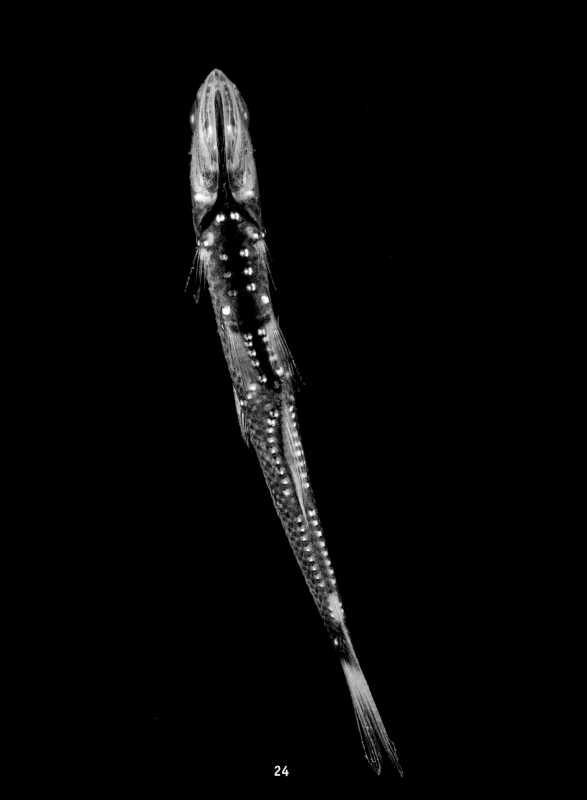

CHAPTER 3

Water Migrations

Rivers, lakes, and oceans are all home to migrating creatures. Some, such as the limpet, migrate just a few feet each day as they follow the tide. Others, such as whales, swim for hundreds or thousands of miles. Lobsters might migrate to avoid bad weather. Other animals travel to breed or give birth.

The lantern fish migrates about 3,000 feet (914 m). It travels from deeper water up to shallower water.

Able to Adapt

Most fish live either in salt water or freshwater. Salmon live in both! They are born in freshwater and swim to the ocean to grow into adulthood. Then they migrate back to their birthplace to lay eggs. As they move between salt water and freshwater, their body changes to suit the environment. A salmon's trip can be hundreds of miles long and very hard. To reach the place where they were born, they must swim against the current of the river.

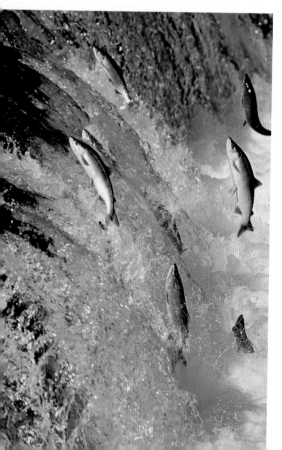

Salmon migrating to their birthplace must occasionally swim up a waterfall!

26

Humpback Whale Migration Routes

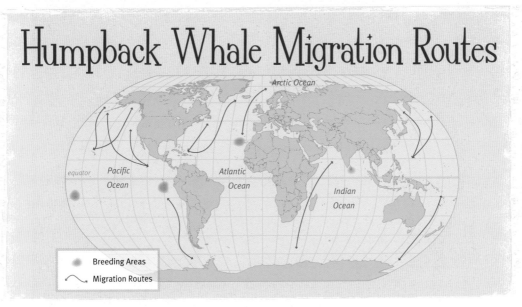

Arctic Ocean

equator | Pacific Ocean | Atlantic Ocean | Indian Ocean

- ● Breeding Areas
- ⌒ Migration Routes

Staying Warm

Humpbacks in the Northern **Hemisphere** migrate south in the winter to warmer waters near the equator. They travel back north in the summer. In the Southern Hemisphere, the whales move north to the warmer winter waters. They migrate south again for the summer.

Humpbacks use their time in warm water to have their babies and eat lots of food. During the cold winter, they stay warm because of their blubber, a layer of fat stored in their body.

Hammerheads use Earth's magnetic field to find their way.

Travel Buddies

Some hammerhead sharks spend their lives inside a defined **home range**. Other hammerheads migrate long distances. Their journey follows the seasons, just as a humpback whale's does. Migrating hammerheads often travel in large groups. A single group can contain hundreds of sharks. They are one of the few sharks to migrate together.

Time for Babies

When a sea turtle lays its eggs, it does something very unusual: It migrates to its natal beach, which is where the turtle was born. This is amazing for two reasons. First, the beach might be thousands of miles from the turtle's current location. Second, it could be 20 years or longer since the turtle was at that beach!

Smells and tastes might help a sea turtle find the beach where it was born.

29

CHAPTER 4

Air Migrations

As warm summer days turn into the chillier ones of autumn, the sky is filled with insects and birds beginning their long journeys south. They know by instinct that they cannot survive in their summer home. Many of these animals have a very hard trip ahead of them. It is common for these animals to deal with predators, bad weather, and not having enough food along the way.

Hummingbirds eat nectar from flowers and must migrate to find it.

Wonder Bug!

Each spring, millions of monarch butterflies migrate north from Florida, Texas, and Mexico. They head to summer homes in Canada and the northern United States, laying eggs along the way. These monarchs live only a few weeks. Their eggs hatch and develop, and the next **generation** of butterflies continues the journey. It takes up to four generations to complete the trip. The last generation lives several months. This single generation will travel the entire migration route south the next fall.

Monarch butterflies gather to rest on their long migration south.

32

Golden eagles usually migrate alone.

Designed for Travel

Golden eagles' bodies are made for long trips. They have strong, lightweight skeletons. Their lungs use oxygen very efficiently. This means their lungs do not need much oxygen to work well. Golden eagles migrate at midday to take advantage of thermals. These are pockets of warm air that help them glide, using less energy to fly. Thermals are strongest during the middle of the day.

Bill Lishman flew a type of small aircraft called an ultralight.

An Amazing Story

Some birds, such as geese, cranes, and swans, learn their migration route from their parents. But what happens to orphaned birds? Can they learn from another bird—or another creature? A man named Bill Lishman helped a group of geese travel safely to a winter home. He convinced the birds that their "mother" was a small, simple airplane. The young geese followed it south. Today, Lishman helps endangered whooping cranes migrate safely.

Nonstop Journey

Have you ever gone for a long run? As you ran farther and farther, you probably became very tired and wanted to stop. Imagine what it is like to be the bar-tailed godwit. When this bird migrates across the Pacific Ocean, it might need to fly for more than a week without stopping! The bar-tailed godwit holds the record for the longest nonstop flight: 7,145 miles (11,500 km) over nine days!

Some godwits fly from Alaska to New Zealand without food or drink.

Air Current Experts

There are six kinds of sandhill cranes. Three kinds migrate. Their winter homes are located in states along the Gulf of Mexico. Some migrating sandhill cranes spend their summers in Minnesota, Alaska, and Canada. Others fly across the Bering Strait to Siberia. Sandhill cranes migrate during the day. They know when to fly higher and when to fly lower to take advantage of warm air and wind speeds. This helps make their journey easier.

Sandhill cranes fly hundreds of miles a day during their migration.

Stopping to Rest

Many animals have certain spots where they stop every year to rest and gain weight. Some sandhill cranes take a six-week break on the Platte River in Nebraska. Monarch butterflies often stop at Stonington Peninsula in Michigan before heading south. La Charca (below) is a pond in the Canary Islands where birds migrating from Europe to Africa like to rest.

CHAPTER 5

Migration Is Hard Work!

The migration journey can be very stressful. Imagine what it would be like to fly, swim, or walk for hundreds or thousands of miles in all kinds of weather! Sometimes animals have a hard time finding enough food to eat along the journey. There are often dangerous predators. A bad storm or strong winds can cause an animal to stop before it had planned to.

Some birds may use a storm's strong winds as a helpful push forward.

As Antarctica warms, the krill that Adélie penguins depend on for food die off.

Big Changes

Many scientists argue that Earth is slowly becoming warmer because of pollution. A warmer Earth could lead to many changes. There might be less polar ice, making it harder for polar bears to travel and find food. Many animals rely on changes in temperature to know when it is time to migrate. If these changes come at the wrong time—or not at all—this could upset migration **cycles**.

Buildings, Lights, and Tall Towers

When people construct buildings, roads, mobile phone towers, and wind turbines, they often destroy important nesting sites and disturb migration routes. These structures can also become obstacles for traveling animals. Bright lights can be confusing to migrating animals, too. For example, sea turtles must head to water right after they are born. They find it by heading to the lighter sky over the ocean. Artificial lights near their nesting sites can cause the turtles to travel in the wrong direction.

The rotating blades of wind turbines can injure migrating birds.

Learning About Migration

Humans have been curious about migration for a long time. In the late 1800s, scientists captured animals to put labeled metal bands on them before releasing them. The scientists hoped people would contact them if they found any of these tagged animals, so they could learn where the animals had gone. It worked! Now scientists rely on tracking devices. These use radio signals to communicate with satellites to let researchers "follow" an animal's movements.

Some tracking chips are small enough to attach to an insect!

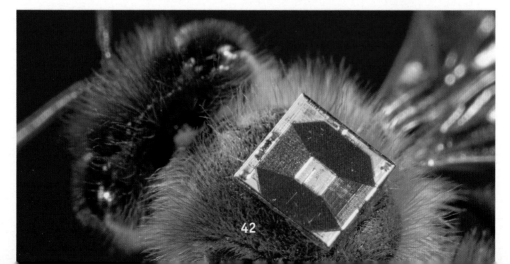

Through education, people are learning the importance of protecting the jaguar in Costa Rica.

Protecting Migration Sites and Routes

Governments, citizens, and developers often work together to protect animal habitats. In Costa Rica, jaguars can migrate through developed areas along the protected "jaguar corridor." In Wyoming, **conservationists** study and protect pronghorn routes. In California, farmers create temporary wetlands where animals can rest along migration routes. With such care and efforts, we can share this world with wonderful animals and ensure their survival. ★

Distance the average Arctic tern travels over the course of its life: 1.5 million mi. (2.4 million km)—the same as three round-trips to the moon!

Insect with the longest migration: Monarch butterfly, traveling up to 3,000 mi. (4,828 km)

Number of wildebeests that migrate across Africa each year: More than 1 million

How long ruby-throated hummingbirds migrate without stopping: 18 to 20 hours

Distance of the humpback whale's migration from Costa Rica to Antarctica: At least 5,100 mi. (8,207 km)

Distance some Chinook salmon migrate: 900 mi. (1,448 km)

Did you find the truth?

F Migrations are always at least 100 miles (161 kilometers) long.

T Humans have been able to teach a flock of birds to migrate.

Resources

Books

Marsh, Laura. *Amazing Animal Journeys*. Washington, DC: National Geographic, 2010.

O'Sullivan, Joanne. *Migration Nation: Animals on the Go from Coast to Coast*. Watertown, MA: Imagine Publishing, 2015.

Parker, Steve. *Extreme Animals*. Hauppauge, NY: Barron's Educational Series, Inc., 2009.

Visit this Scholastic Web site for more information on animal migrations:
★ www.factsfornow.scholastic.com
Enter the keywords **Animal Migrations**

Important Words

conservationists (kahn-sur-VAY-shun-ists) — people who protect forests, wildlife, and natural resources

cycles (SYE-kuhlz) — series of events that are repeated in the same order

extinction (ik-STINGK-shuhn) — the state of no longer being found alive

generation (jen-uh-RAY-shuhn) — all the animals born around the same time

GPS (jee-pee-ES) — short for Global Positioning System, a system of satellites and devices that people use to find out where they are or to get directions to a place

hemisphere (HEM-i-sfeer) — one half of Earth

home range (HOME RAYNJ) — the area in which an animal spends most of its time

magnetic field (mag-NET-ik FEELD) — the area around a magnet or electric current that has the power to attract other metals; Earth has magnetic fields that animals use to navigate

migrate (MYE-grate) — to move to another area or climate at a particular time of year or day

monsoons (mahn-SOONZ) — very strong winds that can cause heavy rains or hot, dry weather

nomadic (noh-MAD-ik) — wandering from place to place

Index

Page numbers in **bold** indicate illustrations.

About the Author

Vicky Franchino lives in a state where it is very cold in the winter. She thinks it would be a good idea for her to start seasonally migrating someplace warm! Vicky has written many books about animals and enjoyed learning more about the different types of migration. She was very surprised to find out that some animals migrate very short distances (read this book to learn more!). Vicky lives in Madison, Wisconsin, with her family.

Photo by Kat Franchino